W0259437

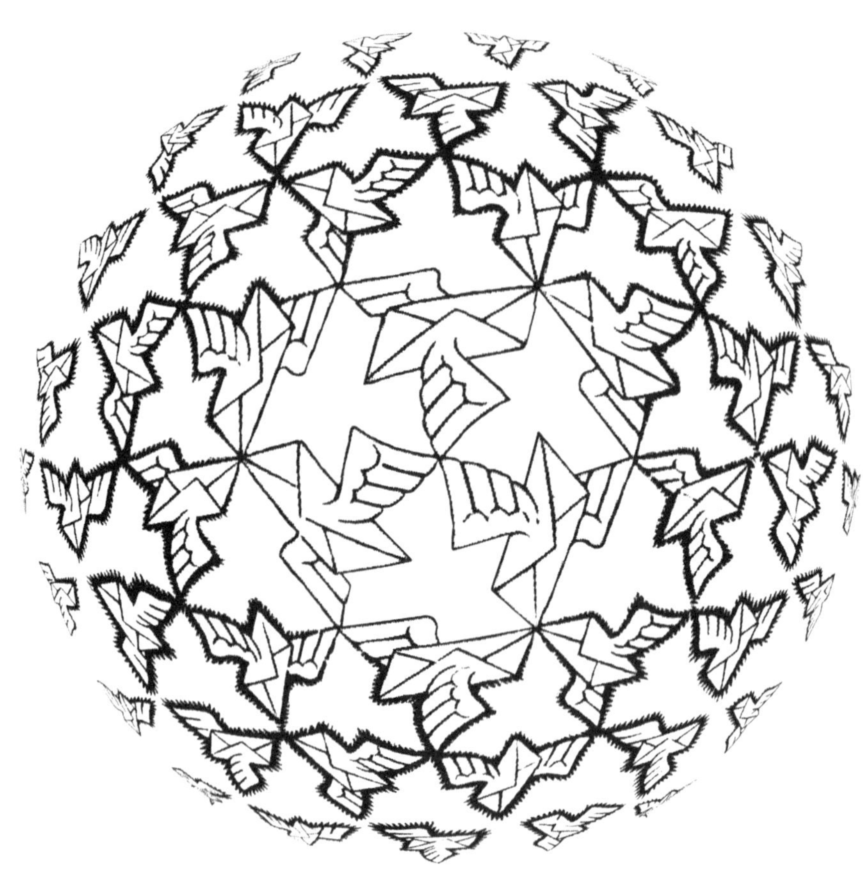

Lines of Embarkation

Stan Rogal

Coach House Books

First Edition

Illustrations by Stan Rogal

CANADIAN CATALOGUING IN PUBLICATION DATA

Rogal, Stan, 1950-
Lines of embarkation

Poems.
ISBN 1-55245-064-3

I. Title.

PS8585.O391L436 1999 C183'.54 C99-932081-5
PR9199.3.R63L436 1999

Special thanks to Douglas R. Hofstædter, whose book *Gœdel, Escher, Bach: An Eternal Golden Braid*, provided much information and inspiration. Not a map, but a network of possibilities. To quote:

As in a fairy tale, to seek self-knowledge is to embark on a journey which … will always be incomplete, cannot be charted on any map, will never halt, cannot be described.

TABLE OF CONTENTS

The world is a complex, continuous, single event.

– Leonard B. Meyer

EMBARK

embark/im-'bark/ *vb* [MF *embarquer*, Fr. OProv *embarcar*, Fr. *em-* (Fr. L *im-*) + *barca* bark] *vt* 1: to cause to go on board a boat or airplane. 2: to engage, enlist, or invest in an enterprise. 1: to go on board a boat or airplane for transportation. 2: to make a start: COMMENCE <~ed on a new career>

Begun.
Perhaps not the best of beginnings.
Still. Having begun impossible not to.

A solid lump of substance will just sit there harmlessly
(say, a lemon or a melon), but:
beyond the critical point, the system suddenly
attains the capacity for self-reference, & thereby
dooms itself to incompleteness

A pretty thot.
Without the threat of a dog barking at one's heels
or a gun to the head.

A critical point is inherent which triggers an explosion

How water knows to freeze at 0° C & boil at 100° C
or uranium becomes a bomb.
Not 'know' that kind of 'know' yet in a limited sense.
I HAVE NEVER HAD AN ORIGINAL IDEA IN MY ENTIRE LIFE.
Unable to step into that same fucking river twice (or once,
even) without picking up something I say I 'know'.
Like, what we name a thing makes a difference.
Why a rose is not a palindrome or a quark or a river
(tho we can image a river of roses, a golden braid of river
flowing deep within the rose).
Why this rose is not this rose.
Or cold water turns hot at the suggestion & raises a welt.
Tricks performed without mirrors & nothing up the sleeve.
Except. The head of this rose with enuf critical energy
to explode any river back to its beginning.
No lemon, no melon.

MOUNTAIN

1 First there is a mountain
replete with crags.
Ledges
rammed tight
the horns twisting
to the dead centres
of it.

There is no thought here
but one imagines.

There is little else.
Still, a vagrant fly
sets the entire scene.
Quaking.
The animals make their ceramic plunge.
Dust circles their footprints.

2 Then there is no mountain.
A line remains but it is hardly the same.
More like a building with elevators.
Windows black beneath the eye of commerce.
The animals have no recollection
of having been animals.
The rocks have no recollection.
Even the line forgets.
Even the line assumes its shape.
The elevator plunges & the motion is ceramic.
No comparison should be made.
There is no sadness & no dust.

3 Then there is.
Not like before but
like before.
It has a voice that speaks mountain
but without the weight.
Without the loneliness.
It plunges forever &
    there is no comparison.
There is only that one word &
everything it entails.

Mountain.
Mountain.
Mountain.

SIGNATURES

The railway stitches a red tear
      running the possible limit of what might be called.
A country.
Who cannot not follow it & remain
Unidentified?
Shoes that image themselves as feet in this dust
Learn to go by going.
This says nothing for the rest.
How split a personality lost invisible beneath such lands-
Cape?
Merlin or any other quest.
Guessed wrongly.
Without the promise of a sword to wrestle from a stone
Few venture from the tracks
Or risk the riddle of monsters hunkered in sand.
Searching for meaning where none was intended
      also has meaning.
As centuries old wheel ruts still signature the plain
& rocks piled neatly one atop the other still scream.
Direction.
Railroaded east to west & west to east
Raises little question.
Outside this narrow frame. The prints of a stranger.
Guessed.

RANDOM CAGES

There is a fracture I am pulled inside out of.
A hairline travelling one end to an other.

More noticeable in the dark since it makes a sound.
One hears only at the point of not listening.

Imaginary Landscape #4 structures music in random cages.
24 performers twiddling 24 knobs on 12 radios: volume & station.

The border between self & the rest impossible to dissolve.
2 lizards locked straining in opposite directions is also music.

Between me & the door the haunted breathing of furniture.
Outside a stranger sloshes moonlight in a pail.

What hand or door records the knock that is not knocked?
Who can say if the hand clenched & the hand open is the same?

If there was no god, it would create one.
Balanced on the edge of this cracked surface without a net.

Rubbing acid into the palms of the hands is a leap in the dark.
Or incautiously throwing open the door I thot I heard myself.
Disappear.

BEARDED EROS

for Louis Zukofsky

The more you understand an age, the more convinced you become that the images a given poet used and which you thot his own were taken almost unchanged from another poet... poets are more concerned with arranging images than with creating them. Images are given to poets; the ability to remember them is far more important than the ability to create them.

– Viktor Shklovsky

1 *advice*
Don't sweat it cats.
Others swoon on
        salty rhyme
embrace love's prick
bunt belying cant
the dull smut
never reaching bone
you'll canter
all it's worth
    no forgetting
    an old flame
    like making
    a new flame
the same tired story

bunt:
push & shove; middle
bellying portion
of a sail or fishnet;
a parasitic fungus,
species of smut
which converts
interior of grains
of wheat
into a black, fetid
powder.

cant:
inclination or tipping;
hypocritical or
ostentatious religious
talk; any technical or
professional jargon;
secret language of
thieves, gypsies, beggars
etc. Scot: bold, brisk,
lively

lit
with a new match
the net licked hot
with fevered tongues:
beggars, gypsies,
thieves.

Art is a way of
experiencing
the artfulness of an
object; the object
is not important.

– Shklovsky

The ghosts you secrete are worms eager for fish.

But defamiliarization is not only a technique
of the erotic riddle – a technique of euphemism –
it is also the basis and point of all riddles.

– Shklovsky

Bull by the horn old cock!
Give it & go on giving
Catullus
    who'll have it.

2 *response* (a free translation from a poem by Catullus)

Catullian: *A satisfactory style is precisely that style which delivers the greatest am't of thot in the fewest words.*

Aristotle: *Poetic language must appear strange & wonderful.*

By 'works of art,' in the narrow sense, we mean works created by special techniques designed to make the works as obviously artistic as possible.

– Shklovsky

Malest, Cornifici, tuo Catullo,
Malice – Cornificius – your Cats'
malest, me hercule, et ei laboriose,
malicious for some stud's labours.
et magis magis in dies et horas
Make it, make it any day now some hour?
quem tu, quod minimum facillimumquest,
Get off! What an easy quest.
qua solatus es allocutione?
Consolation for lack of allocation?
irascor tibi. sic meosamores?
Air I score baby! Make me sick or amorous?
paulum quid lubet allocutionis
Poor this lame love is, all cute ones
maestius lacrimis Simonideis.
mist as tears miss my poor Lesbia.

SHAPING

trapped by my shaping
the impingement of form
upon my self &

                              outside

                      the world
surrounds me like a line
defines me   my shape
compresses me
the expanse of my body anchors me
grounds me in the world
my voice is strangled & disguised
when I scream
the sound crashes against my form
ricochets back
stunsmebruisesmekeepsme
captive
              deep
within my skin

LAUGHING MATTER

Fuguing around jars some bottled laughter from some.
Groans from others groan up not knowing.
When a door is not a door.
Groan tall as that groan man you can't bear to see cry.
Though you would like to.
Groan for obvious reasons.
Armed
        with would nots
        no bare can sink its teeth
                or slip a would in edgewise.
Honey.
The games we played as kids way baaa-ck
        before the would had groan flesh.
'Horny as a goat' was simply woods to be disentangled
        just as an 'ass-hole' became a place to bury a dead donkey.
'Penis' was someone who played piano.
        'Vagina' was a city in Saskatchewan.
                'Getting laid' was something an egg did.
Laughing our fool heads off.
One girl split a gut.
A brother died of it.
Laughter.
Nothing so serious as this, saying:
This is no joke.
This is 'the bare shit in the woulds.'

PILE OF BONES

Who swallows all the rocks & mountains
    & spits them out again to be seen, finally.
Would make a group of seven cry.
Not a map with its flat relief & empty legends
    but lines that threaten to rupture at any moment
        & show displeasure at the indifference of insects.
How scale this wolfish bark content to box itself in canyons?
Keeping the moon captive in a pail of water by the door
    settles a town that defends things as they are
        because they are refusing to give ground.
An interest past potatoes.
Madly howling when rowers rowing through dust
    begin to resemble landscape & vice versa.
The embalmed everyday claiming each city 'Pile of Bones'.
Lying at the heart of no mystery.
The railroad brought the first & lasting lyric.
Passengers hypnotized by that dead refrain.
Faces imbedded in glass.
Rifles leaning cocked from their eyes.
Sights set forever on the same mindless game.
When she saw the name on the sign she laughed
    'It's not on the map,
        so it doesn't exist.'
Shifting domains.
Who would recognize the moon
    given all this distance.

ÉTUDE

The thing made is a network.
Like *no lemon, no melon* reads the same.
Forever. Backward & forward.
Action providing a tonic to unscramble cryptic notes
        that fail to designate sounds overflowing
                the boundaries of their measure.
The crude eye is charmed by some such magic &
        beauty crawls from the clash of savage beasts.
E fish in C, for example, is not
        a Bach fugue or instructions to anglers.
(Tho it is not, necessarily, not, either).
As if to image Chopin alive at 49.
Coughing up notes not scaled in blood
        was enuf to provoke a simple variation on a theme
                none could refuse to listen to &
Understand. As the struck moon.
Drawn from thin air & splashed in the bucket by the door
        affords some mutilated music thru reappearance.
Begins a descending slide of infinite proportion.
The tongue hunting out a missing key
        from a lover's mouth so filled with locks & chains
                no logic can escape or break the silent chord.
Only the hand tilting with the beat of wings
        colours this strange execution
Strangely
Chromatic.

HE ROSE

for Bertolt Brecht

Searching out HE ROSE from anonymous history.
This is the final breach of faith.
Arriving as they do with no one left to collect their tears.
In a bucket kicked or otherwise.
Without a bridge of asses to mirror this guarded angle.
One world to the next & no word remaining
    to cup the blood of five drained roses
        & maintain HE ROSE.
Poor this poor people is that lacks.
Poorer still that needs.
HE ROSE. With *pons asinorum* a prayer upon the lips.
& each glass blushes rose & turns its face to the wall.
A stone so heavy even God can't lift.
Only the moon.
Pissing its soft yellow liquid
    through the branches
        breaking up against the rocks.
In fits. Laughing, said:
HE ROSE. & kicking,
    kicked the bucket.

TEMPUS FUGIT

for Count Leo Tolstoy

2:30 am
2:40 am

That was the quickest ten minutes I never saw.
Or a lifetime.
Passes *as tho never lived*.
Chief Tall Story preached to a pack of mushers
        too thick with birdlime & mistletoe
                to measure the flow of this novel direction.
Rooted by an arbitrary number
of such magnitude
no change of temperature could lower resistance
        or rouse from cushioned sleep
                beyond the bark of appetites.
No place in this garden for woods that will not bend.
When existence under shear stress becomes second nature
Tundra percolates the great cavity of the trunk
        & internal organs turn to stone.

2:41 am
(But, many years later …)

SKATERS

In my head skates the story of a tiny policeman
Telling the story of a tiny policeman skating in my head.
In his head too skates the same story
Told by an even tinier policeman.
& so on.
Until there is no longer any need to tell it.
Any need to listen.
There is, then, only the story.
Skating past all notion
There ever was:
    a skater
    a tiny policeman
    a surging sheet of ice
Skating past all notion
There ever was
A story.

ICE AGE

improvisation on a line by Brassai

Reaching for the brass eye
one man can destroy an entire city.

Technology makes each of us a capable god.
So much for miracles.
In Toronto everyone walks on water
  & fish divide themselves like playing cards
    across the slick shoreline.
Cannon fire dredged the last handsome drowned body
  from the guts of this lake ages ago.
Nothing supports this departure.
Unable & unwanting to turn back the clock.
Counting beans with Thoreau.
Stooped day after day on mom's home-fry & mint juleps.
A summer spent chasing loons & scant pages of virgin snow.
Flakes romantically imaged:
  chariot wheels fallen from a battle in the sky.
Ignoring pillars of ice (the largest on record)
  calving into bays of disenchantment. Here,
(alone), exists the hoary fear that words
    carry the contagion of misfortune.
Who hears ten tens in the centarians.
Nothing more.
& knots the end of this thread around a finger
  in order not to remember
    not not to forget.
Destroys.

VOLCANO

Sunday May 18/80. First sun finds the mountain still.
Drowsing.

Living in the shadow of this mountain range
nurtures a race of sleepwalkers.

What might be the Himalayas floats on the surface like rum on
Coke to fool the senses. Cushioned on clouds or bubbles mainly
CO_2 & water vapour seeming harmless by all appearances.

As well, the tulip replaces the lotus with the same effect.
Visions of sugar plums dancing in an untended garden.

The lion sleeps with the grouse & the salmon never
meet themselves coming & going in this looped space.

Call it a life, afraid to wake & find the hands pinning them
to the mountain sides are their own, even as the mountain
prepares to shake off its skin & plummet into hell.

Equivalent to 10 megatons of TNT. More than 5000
times the am't dropped in the great raid on Dresden,
Germany in 1945. Made up mostly of carbon dioxide
& water vapour, innocuous except when under the
terrible pressure & heat of a volcano's insides & then
suddenly released.

This is the critical point driving home thru illusion.
The signs simply vanish.

The multichrome, three dimensional world of trees,
hill & sky becomes a monochrome of powdery grey ash …
blotting out horizons & perception of depth.

Poetry & prose cascade in random heaps along with birds,
fish & animals.
Perish.

DRAGONS

Babysitter Laurie Dann's descent into madness began long before she opened fire on a class of second graders.

– *People* Weekly, June 6, 1988

Well out of harm's way.
Somewhere not on the bus schedule, fer sure.
Not in a hospital where more people die than anywhere.
Or:
    '… an idyllic community where parents knew
        their children were safe …'
A place where legs grow long enough to reach the ground
    & no longer.
Where no one risks asking God to create a rock
    even God can't lift. This is contentment.
Reason for a well-defined system
    boxes a dragon in parts that
        finally grows tired of chasing its own tale.
Bent on roasting the old monologue to death.
Flashing RED YELLOW GREEN symbols
    everyone is meant to understand & obey.
The colour-blind recognizing order, the blind
satisfied with sounds mainly YELLOW.
At any rate feeling safe between parallel lines
    bathed in a calming glow of green.
No square for any serpent riddled in flames. Except.
The form of lower Eden triggers a small town
    toward the massacre of innocents.
Later to be cribbed an isolated incident
    ignoring the fact   only the freak
Endures.
Children hung from the beard of the garden dwarf.

They lock the doors upon themselves while up the stairs
every attic maintains
its steady grind
of steel
on stone.

PORTRAIT OF THE ARTIST IN A FLOWERED HAT

Unmistakably an Ensor, but,
    what was the quest on?
To create from the already created
    creates a small 'i' &
        makes an ordinary cabbage obscene.
Rembrandt badly hung in this bad light.
This mirror mirrored in the eyes of mirror critics
    bound by strict laws of reflection
        teeming just above the mere surface.
Difficult to pity all airless, closed faces, writing:

        x of x': 'We find much of your work offensive'
        y of y': 'The work strikes us as somewhat contrived'
        z of z': 'Derivative & pretentious '

Where skeletons fight over the body of a hanged man
& eggplants scale their snowy breasts with strands of gold.
Allowing.
It takes more than a man, a horse & a meat grinder
    to birth a Centaur. I admit nervousness seeing:

        a red wheelbarrow
        glazed in rain water
        surrounded by white
        chickens.

Shit.
The blue rider leaps into the glassy pond.

VOWELS

I breathe the same air Rimbaud breathed.
Don't I.
Breathe.
Like, those pretty painted vowels
Want to go on forever, man.
But the breath runs out of legs.
Faithless as this.
Why.
Or a consonant making the scene
With its shaved head &
    bulging leathers
Kicked shit out of poor
Insubstantial
You.
Trumpeting harsh with strange
Silent
Oh.
The violet light of his eyes.
Gone crazy in this black wood, man.
Gone crazy.
Gone.
Oh.
The violent, oh,
Night
Of his
Thighs.

ZENO'S PARADOX

The first letter of
any poem
    is always 'a'.
Comfort (even) for an old Greek.
Zeno, for instance, would applaud.
Such immutability. Such endless non-progression.
Never reaching halfway until half way to halfway
    & halfway to halfway to halfway & et cetera, etc.
Achilles lost at the starting line
    where a fleet forward step would
        boil any distanced turtle to plodding soup.
Puzzled by the shortness of his own mean feat
    to disentangle from this literal knot. Or:
Held fast between Scylla and Charybdis
    rearranges itself to mean
        web scented, can hardly sail by.
Not hardly, Achilles, but unable.
Ground bombed by halves & halves remains uncaptured.
The same general rule applies.
    'The ampersand sign' is
        'met reshaping "ands"'
& more specifically
'a poem'
also
begins with
'"a"'

AHA

The problem like some language from Mars constructs:

Ship (x) moving NE 17° at 20 knots/hr.
Smoke (y) rising from the stack at 5 knots/hr.
Wind (z) blowing SW 35° at 15 knots/hr.
In what direction & at what speed does the
smoke travel?

Rather cross a burning bridge of asses
    mapping one angel to another
        than wrestle this dragon from its box.
Or, unasking the question, say: 'It is not Buddha'
    gets an 'F' & no escaping proper method, except.
Who answers rightly doesn't rightly think.
Gazing goo-goo eyed before a window snaps
    AHA knowing out-of-the-blue this & further beasts.
The perverse product of grotesque numbers.
The gross head of cattle grazing in a field.
The numbers of beans stuffed inside a jar plus or minus.
Who stutters, has chronic itch, a pimply nose, warts,
    shits his jeans when excited or confused
        could've been anyone but wasn't is
A Lesson In Biology.
Without meaning to fill the gap.
Fails math adding 6 & 8 is 68.
Fails literature figuring Gogol is 10^{100}
Fails history estimating 1729 the sum of two cubes.
Fails to see the humour:
    Why did 6 hate 7?
        Because 789.
Nowhere near out-of-the-blue. He
    shits his jeans.

GOODBYE

Dear diary.
This was leaving home after all.
Not wishing on a star or sucked unawares
by a tornado but real unfucking packed.
Lock, stock & barrel.
Barely enough to fill the trunk of a car.
A small car.
The things that identify a life.
A portable Smith-Corona typewriter with well-used ribbon.
2 suitcases containing clothes, toothbrush et cetera
& 4 books:
Cortazar's *Hopscotch*.
Genet's *Our Lady of the Flowers*.
Rimbaud's *Collected Works*.
Spicer's *Collected Books*.
Only room for a couple of dead bastards.
Destined for no desert island
        practical underwear replaced
                the proverbial 6 others.
A few cassettes. Some broken oil pastels.
Coloured pencils. X-Acto knife. Glue.
Set squares. The dimensions of the Great
Egyptian Pyramid.
What was I planning?
A photo of my best friend giving me the finger.
Not much to show for 36 years.
A few bucks in the bank.
Saving on air fare flying the red eye.
No job.
No star.
Vancouver to Toronto non-stop. 4 1/2 hours &
a woman waiting on the other end.

The only guarantee.
Drinking all day beginning with beer
then into the wine
working on rum & Cokes about the time
I was dragged off to grab a meal
surprised with a party of friends & family
everyone wanting to buy me a drink
1, 2, 3, 5, 9, et cetera, a row of 'em, all
doubles
making it to the airport just before pumpkin hour
3 sheets to the wind. Everyone goofy as hell.
People crying, hugging, kissing, shaking hands
meanwhile the plane
pushing me forcibly thru the gate saying
goodbye, goodbye
my brothers mooning me from the window
their bare asses squashed against the glass.
Unreal as a dish of Escher ice-cream
one thing melting fuzzily into another.
Feeling like some character in a crazy Hollywood flick
about the innocent & groovy sixties.
If I look at my feet I'll be wearing one glass slipper
& the credits will roll. There'll be music.
Simon & Garfunkel singing, 'Mrs. Robinson'
The Lovin' Spoonful doing 'You're a Big Boy Now.'
I couldn't stomach that.
I'd puke for sure.
Meanwhile the camera pans the crowd.
Close-up of the bare asses.
The lonely hallway.
The plane.
Moving backwards across the runway.
Shot of the night sky.

Stars.
Moon.
Credits rolling but I can't see my name.
Music playing but I can't make out the tune.
Goodbye. Goodbye.
Maybe something about a rainbow.
About a bird.
I'm on the jog. Bouncing wall to wall.
Having to piss like a racehorse.
Goodbye. Goodbye.
I make it to my seat.
I buckle in.
I look down at my feet.
Runners, thank Christ. 2 of 'em.
We're in the air. I use the head.
I wash my face.
I look in the mirror until
I see something I recognize.
Yeah. That's it.
I go to my seat.
I order a rum.
I don't look out the window.
I close my eyes & breathe.
Just breathe.
Goodbye.
Goodbye.
Goodbye.

BOXED

RACE HATRED EXPLODES ON US COMMUNITY TV
'Race & Reason' opens with soft, insistent music …

– *The Toronto Star*, August 19, 1988

Exists a gap between the thing & its name
No god can fill.
This is where the bottom drops out
      & vision ends.
All kind creatures in the subnuclear zoo
Drained of all redeeming blood.
Allowing ungrand dragons public access to the box
      breeds hellfire beyond the swaggered jimmy
            of a few devoted locks.
Rips the drawers from every armless subject
      then fires straight from the hip.
Levelling a race & leaving reason to burn from a cross.
Setting the illusion of stepping outside itself.
Forgets.
That shadowy tattoo that haunts the bottoms of the feet.
Enuf to shake the very walls
      & box every narrow dragon madly
Swallowing its own
Tail.

LADY LINDY

for Richard Brautigan

What becomes a legend most?
50 days in 50 cities
Thanking God & the Wright Bros.
1729 became 1927 overnight &
    'The American Ambassador of good will'
        unscrambled to headline:
            'a dramatic solo woos Lindbergh a fame.'
Fleeting. Like that big trout that got away.
Who crossed the Atlantic a year later
    in 20 hours & 40 minutes produced:
        a book
        a series of lectures
        a line of women's clothing
        a nickname that haunted her for 9 years.
Flying higher & faster than any other woman.
Going down November 3, 1970 Dick left
    the Amelia Earheart Pancake Poem
Half-flipped.
Like that other mission.
Crash-landed in a rice paddy just north of Hope.
Lost forever in those strange woods.
'Bullets,' cried the trout,
    'are such a fleeting thing. More fleeting than fame.
        More fleeting, even, than we
Trout.'

STILL

Two inconsequential things can come together
to become a consequence.

– Jack Spicer

A retired sailor is a seagull
with one leg balanced at the end of a pier.
Waiting.
The sailor waits for his ship to come in.
The seagull waits for what is offered.
In the attitude of a child.
Between them, the forgotten bait.
Beyond is the ocean.
Each side conceals its emptiness. Its danger. Its fear.
Still. The bait is real &
the gull leans from one eye.
No poison can deter this craving.
Still. The cast of a ship
hooks a second eye.
No ghost can deter this longing.

At the edge of this ocean
a child wanders unaffected.
Still.

TANTALUS

Who murders sleep deals in nightmares.
Devillers who formulate stranger creatures
    dwelling in the syntax than
        roam the false bottom of the La Brea Tar Pits
Contend with the 5 most petrified woods in the English lang-
Scape: Time, People, Water, Way & Words.
The heads of a nation buried in muck.
Remaining well back of the edge. Simple thots turn
Criminal.
Moebius locked in the rib-cage of a dinosaur.
Unable to count on a lover's kiss to supply the key.
Here, the divinity of poets & the shaping force of nature
Cease to exist.
King Zalm displaying 20 year old snaps to tourists
    now bare of foliage while
        the life of Brian unfolds a Gucci in every pot
& an axe & shovel for every man, woman & child.
Enuf lumber to last 700 years fell in less than a lifetime.
What journey takes a hero home that lacks a forest?
That destroys any chance of a redeeming dragon?
Feeling there is no burden too heavy but
    there's a man to pull it assumes that
        beyond these fuzzy mountains breathe
More mountains.
A modifier dangled just out of reach
That transfigures children to stone
To test the powers of the gods
Pulls the bottom falsely out from under.
No path leading nowhere for no experience. Only this
Fall. This failing
To wrestle sleep from these slumbered bones.

STORY

A point being the intersection of two lines.
& a line being the extension of one point to another.
We are led back to no beginning.
The bare particle threatens by its very unexistence.
There is no frame beyond this fact. Every beast
makes itself up in small copies then seeks its complement.
One hand draws the other whether in Crete or Toronto.

This is the story:

    If the Minotaur never lived it never died.
    A string to tie to the end of a knot.
    Or, what begins & ends with 'he'
    past the power of any god
    is a headache.

Ariadne would discover this too late.
Hooked by that old played-out line.
Amazing Theseus drawn by the thread of a myth &
    hanging by a hair between two fates.
Defining each by the other. Mirrors threatening to tilt
    against monster windmills
        set within sets of hypothetical boxes
            each one larger & more powerful than the last.
The Minotaur rubbed its Buddha belly & puzzled:
    'What knotted word that contains four letters
        A-D-A-C consecutively, HeHe?'
Intent on blood Theseus unasked the question
    with a stroke of his sword
        & again with Ariadne who virtually flickered
            when he raped her
                in & out of existence.

This act transcends the edge of plain strings.
It edges toward the real.
Theseus running off to marry the Queen of the Amazons
taking the cash, the car & the Minotaur's head
as a hood ornament.
Ariadne abandoned along the lakeshore to fend for herself.
Picked up by a young god Bacchus who dries her eyes,
wipes her nose, then fucks her
in the back seat of his red Mercedes.

Though this is what actually happened:

Theseus had his balls chopped by a dyke Amazon with one tit.
Bacchus discovered Ariadne standing in the middle of an
intersection crossed by five streets, the traffic weaving
around her, her sun-drenched hair livened with the
impression of fiery snakes, her voice screeched &
garbled as if a dozen languages were fighting to free
themselves from cut glass. Bacchus was a
Grade-B movie mogul specializing in horror
flicks. He signed her up on the spot & made her a star.
If you look close, you can see her still. Flickering
in the night. Leaving audiences petrified.
Their nerves strung out in knots.

No. This is the story:

TO FORM

I lack strength
to form
the circle
either comes or
goes
the line arcs or
doesn't
the difficulties exhaust me
the circle is unreasonable
the sphere
impossible

TOTEMS

Smash the compasses.
Burn the maps.
With ears tuned to the burrowed prey
    & skin alive to the flow of seasons
        a crystal in the brain magnets all points
North.
True or false.
There is no escaping this icy flow
    with or without totems bearing
RED YELLOW GREEN
    (RED being at the top we learn to recognize first
    colours every movement YELLOW a token colour meant
    to offer choice invariably means stop even GREEN
    blinks caution)
Flashing lights confuse with their indefiniteness
    while a GREEN arrow indicates right of way
UNLESS the intersection is jammed.
    "   a second car is running the red.
    "   a pedestrian.
    "   a dog.
    "   otherwise posted.
We call this traffic control & has nothing to do
    with a sense of movement.
Crowds in Tokyo negotiate differently from
    crowds in Toronto & a tourist is pegged
        beyond the tacky shorts, sunglasses & camera.
Like, the Eskimo having over 500 names for snow
    but none for sand fails to see himself coming & going
        one blind-white dune seeming the same as another
            stuffs the swirling crystals into his mouth
naming it: *the-snow-that-is-not-snow*.

ECHOES

If you steal from one author, it's plagiarism;
if you steal from many it's research.

– Wilson Mizner, in John Burke's *Rogue's Progress,*
quoted from *The New International Dictionary of Quotations*

Who centres the universal wheel?
This line
    is arbitrary
        & smacks of derivation.
Just as Shakespeare
Smacked
    drawing on renewable re-
Sources.
With will to turn the common weal
Grotesque
Ah, rose
    becomes a horse in this magic
Kingdom.
Advancing Grimmelhausen & commedia dell'arte.
To Sterne & Jean Paul & on to James Joyce.
Fischart's style echoes in Bonaventura's *Nachtwacher*.
In Valerio in Buchner's *Leonce & Lena*
    & in the speeches of Zus Bunzli. To these add:
Morgenstern. To these wheel Ensor
Wheeling under Bosch, Brueghel, Poe, Balzac, Heine,
    Baudelaire, Cervantes, Rabelais, Hals, Rembrandt,
        Goya, Watteau, Daumier, Delacroix, Millet, Manet,
    Constable, Turner & Callot. To these spin Nietzsche,
Freud & Jung.
With Picasso
    the silverware was safe.

Not so
    the patterns
        on the wallpaper.
Strange shapes suggest themselves
    & monsters emerge from such strange foliage.
Figures from fairy tales who bar your way
    & demand answers to puzzles long since forgotten.
Called Brownian by some, MU by others
    where motion unexists except
        as a lock
            on the gateless
Gate.

Who centres the universal wheel?
We'll Ensor:
    The oak tree in the garden.

PICK UP THAT MOUNTAIN

How do you sink the Canadian navy?
Put it in water.

A Canadian cannot play the part of a Canadian.
Just so.
A Brit maybe. Or a Yank, who sez:
      'Pick up that mountain & bring it to me.'
Doesn't blink.
Or snatches a river from its bed
      twists the ends
            & smokes it like a marijuana cigarette
has some damn good notion
where the bear shit in the woods.
Imaging a Mountie mushing thru snow
      where neither before existed is also.
All so.
Heroic.
To a country settled in green.
Drawers pull empty from this canvas
      while in the background
James Dean.
In the hide of a cow.
Unable to attract flies
      or mumble an illuminating 'Moo!'
Bursts into flames.

FROM THE BLEACHERS

The trick is always to get to first.
Steal second, sacrifice to third & force home.
A winning diamond scored with logic & guts.
Though even this pales. A walk is unimpressive
    where striking out excites a roar.
Few can outrace the throw to second so never try.
A line drive works. The idea being
    go for the big one. Always.
'That's the name of the game,' said my dad.
A hero or a bum.
'My grandmother can hit chicken-shit Texas Leaguers
    from her rocker all day long.'
Those lazy pineapples floating precise arcs &
    dropping safely between fielders.
Like those Chinese acrobats become a bore
    balanced on the head of a pin
        without the possibility of death.
Just as Vancouver was thrashed by Hawaii.
Numbers proving the effect of such systematic slaughter.
Not the bloodshed but the manner was unsportly.
'Pirhana,' said my dad, 'are kinder to their victims.'
& more entertaining.
We left in the 7th inning stretch.

LUNAR LANDSCAPE

The moon gets sore.
Sometimes. Tired
of hauling tides &
love
    up by the boot-
straps. Tired
of playing mirror
to the preening sun.
The moon gets sore.
Sometimes. & rages.
Squeezing juice from
    every blood-orange
brain.
Dancing each fool's tongue
    with an icy-blue
flame.
The moon gets sore.
Sometimes. & re-
verses:

Did I do, O God,
did I as I said I'd do?
Good,

I did!

THE SOUND

This is the sound. The harp.
Seals muse on the lips of tragic rocks.
Dismembered as a song of Orpheus against the surf.
Surprised, surely, as I was.
That day.
Taking apart the radio
& discovering only wires
Glass tubes & dust. Where,
I wondered,
    was the music?
Even the charm of Bardot's bra failed to ring.
Nor could the sirens' feverish breasts
    stir madness from the cold brains of mudskippers
        strapped too long to their weathered masts.
Listen. The invisible becomes visible in this violet light.
The bloodied head of Orpheus floating on a bellows.
Struck dumb.
In all this
Cool
Blue
Sound.

WITCH OF AGNESI

Witch of Agnesi/-an-'ya-ze/ [Maria Gaetana *Agnesi* 1799 It. mathematician; probably from its resemblance to the outline of a witch's hat]: a plane cubic curve that is symmetric about the y-axis, approaches the x-axis as an asymptote, and has the equation x2y=4a2(2a-y).

Your flight begins low
casual
then rising
swelling like a wave
you arc the moon
reach a peak
&
sensing the symmetry
descend
drawn toward the pattern
of a curve
beautiful in its simplicity
you ride it out
the line perfect
the equation complete

MYTH

Hell between naked & nude
    saying 'naked' displays itself
        we shoot 'nudes'.
Persephone framed in the unseasoned garden.
Naked to the world was not nude.
Plainly stripped bare by a bachelor
    who was no saint mounted shot full of arrows.
Eros aimed through the lens of Venus
    advanced straight for the shaft. Love-drugged
at one level so not responsible is base fact.
The torn dress, the exposed barely nippled breast,
    the terror in the eyes at the moment of forced
        penetration, the enthusiasm of the audience, this
is hard porn no soft focus can escape.
The rest is myth.
Beauty dragged down through tiers
    while tears shed from a mother rashly
        transform flesh to leather seeking direction.
Speech drowned in water with a maid's girdle for a tongue.
The soiled film looping strangely out of sync
    Demeter stuffs her crotch with weeds & brambles
        and brought dark ruin down on men and cattle.
No power above or below able to un-say the innocent world
    or image it otherwise. The gods, too, bound on
        this ill-fated rock.
For the sake of seven blood-purpled seeds.
Six months naked.
Six months nude.

THE LESSON

Learning to keep your nose behind the ball.
Until it snaps.
Otherwise a red flag thrown from the hip
signals
      a penalty
Whistles
      the play
            off-side &
                  an automatic loss
            of
      5
Yards.
This determines what follows.
Depending on down.
Depending on distance.
Depending on time remaining.
      Everything depending upon …

      (no particle ever defined w/o reference to all other
      particles whose def'ns in turn depend on the first
particles)

the old man calling for his favourite
      last second, long yardage play:
            a halfback draw requiring skill, timing &
                  some am't of guts, the runner
            invariably
      gets hit back of the line & my dad yells
'Bum!'
Throws his hands into the air at the thot of a Hail Mary.
'You call that playing football? That's not football.
      That's pissing at the moon.'

My brother & I meanwhile on our feet with the crowd
Follow
    the ball's
        breathless flutter
            into the end-zone, see the tip,
        the bobble, the mad scramble,
    the pile on, the referee's extended arms,
TOUCHDOWN!
Us joining in the roar while he sits.
Forever fashionably unfashionable
    knocks back a last rum & Coke
        grabs us by the wrists packing, sez:
            'You figure it out. Make me sick.
        Cheer for a team
    that plays like a
Violin.'
Him leaving sixty bucks a winner
    having bet BC on the points &
        Saskatchewan on the spread
            swears at the traffic snarling the gate
        tells us to get out of the car & move
    the barricade.
We slip along the emergency road
    & head for daylight
Breaking clean
As a whistle.

RAIN

When the rain comes.

What could be a story by Somerset Maugham.
In Toronto it falls perpendicular
striking perfect circles in the rough walk
that disappear abstractly down gutters
& are taken by the sea.

They run & hide their heads.

Or a painting by Escher.
In Vancouver it hangs in the air
bending light to its liquid way
that weds the rippled surface
& branches go crazy with the moon.

Might as well be dead.

A photograph.
In any city haunted by the strain of this strange rain
walking upon unstill waters
that print a giant's steps
& twists a flooded wreck beyond proportion.

WATERLINES

Water seeks its own level then quits.
Peter's principle remaining a solid rock.
Who denied before the cock crowed. Once
Upon a time there was nothing but water.
& no word to betray a simple stone.

GROUND ZERO

With I at the centre.
Here becomes a well-chosen simplicity.
The sun, for instance. Rises
    & sets precisely as it should.
The good moon slips its liquid chains.
Horizons roll flatly to the edge & no further
    while a mountain or a tree seem forever.
This is the way with mirror folk.
Misrecognizing walls for wilderness
    allows no room to breathe a cursed regrouping.
Every eye strolls unamazed without the threat of threads
    to tangle any misshapen
Minotaur.
Meanwhile skulls line the windows of the unpredictable
    kitchen & Ophelia paces with the wisdom of Solomon.
Half a bloody child pressed sucking at her breast.
Given such a frame greenness dissolves.
Past the fear of bombed ground a simple glass of water
    turns sinister & waves break to toads upon the beach
        destroying hedges & dragging granite blocks into the sea.
A gulf so wide between the self & the rest
Only vermin dare enter. Musing:

        Once, I felt so alone, I thot I didn't exist

& then it went away.
& then I went away.

S10
-3541

BLUE ROSE

for Charles Baudelaire

Calling for an aesthetic of the unexpected.
Wearing the Fool's coat to be other than.
Coughs up toads &
    shits flocks of starlings
Singing from his asshole
    to conjure amuse.
Body layers boxed with rats & further dragons
Defies decoration.
As crystal burns an icy flame &
    refuses to break but shatters
        on lines & laws of its own.
This heart.
So far from any home
No absinthe could make fonder
Operates within a fracture.
The image appearing for its mere effect
    & giving rise to other.
Images.
As this rose
Arose thru violence so purple
    the petals slashed the eyes of any passing glance.
Ecstatic red visions no saint
    shot full of Eros could hope to blossom
Or arouse. Only B.
Grinding sparks between his knees & the concrete
    flickered a thorny blue instant &
        unbreaking
Shattered.

TNT

TNT needed to blast some unidentified type.
To form a proper boarder. No reservations
& cash in advance.
Otherwise it is a wasteland.
Waiting for the axe to fall:

If you speak I will cut off your head.
If you don't speak I will cut off your head.

An intense resolution.
The ears of every beast untriggered by a wind
scaled with cones keyed in ancient tonical rhythms.
A dilemma. The earth upheaving their feet
stuck in the grass or clutching branches.
Unable to disconnect Zen from Zeno.
Alice drank the lemonade, stroked the lemur,
ran with the lemmings & would've lost her head
except for nonsense.
No such uninvited ghost to deal with monsters
banked high in timber.
Whether Madagascar, Norway or BC.
When the landscape disappeared beneath them.
They disappeared.

LEVIATHAN

On the sands of the Texas Gulf Coast, volunteers collected 307 tons of litter, two-thirds of which was plastic, including 31,733 bags, 30,295 bottles & 15,631 six-pack yokes.

– *Time* Magazine, August1988

Look!
That styrofoam cup.
There.
Upturned on the water.
See how it bobs

          back & forth
     back & forth
          back & forth

So white
A passing gull cries up its heart.

 Thecup
 Though
 Hardly
Notices.

Its white ear deaf to the surround of blue sound.
So close to beauty one might venture.
A poem.
A photo.
The opening frames of a foreign film.
None fathoms a shadow
     cast taller than any beast
          swimming in that deep ocean.

Stretching its plastic net to encompass every shore.
Sucking the oxygen from each main vein, each artery.
Hauling fluke, flounder, yellowtail, dolphin,
    even whales fouled with blisters & craters
        their carcasses washed up rotting on the beach.
How easily slaughter turns to laughter at the thot.
A single white cup in all that sound.
Broke up against the rocks in fits. Laughing.

'What did Delaware boys? What did Delaware?'
'She wore a string of pelicans hung 'round her
pretty neck, sir. That's what Dela wore.'

That's what Dela wore.

A SHORT BIO

I've passed the age of Christ. Thank Christ.
Uncrucified. In possession of all my parts
    & no cancer
        that shows.
Feeling well generally. Back problem requiring some care.
From separate childhood accidents a scar
    on the third knuckle of the right pointing finger
        & a scar on my forehead.
Also a scar above my left nut from a hernia operation.
No broken bones. No extraordinary diseases.
No trouble breathing. Blood pressure normal.
Good veins. No allergies. Subject to colds.
My bowels perform more or less regularly & my
    urine ranges from pale to bright yellow, depending.
At any rate, no tenderness or pain.
I drink but don't smoke.
I have a beard.
I am balding.
I am slightly underweight.
I have one false tooth.
I am not quite 6' tall.
I must wear glasses to drive.
I am left-handed.
None of this is serious.
My concerns I consider quite normal. You fill in the blanks.
I mean, is it necessary to say:
    I don't want no nuclear war.
    I don't want no rain that melts thru the rooftops.
    I don't want to eat no fish that glows in the dark.
Yes. It is necessary & more.
Doing the best possible in this impossible world
another poor bastard among poor bastards

needing to pay the rent raise a family buy groceries learn a hundred different ways to serve hamburger disguise a potato decide right from wrong good from bad true from false love from fuck create a seeming life make time for a good time do the good works hope you are not one of the ill-fated 1 out of 4 or 2 out of 3 or drown in the tub or hit by a car or lose your mind or kill yourself or get into prison for a crime you didn't commit or have a child you don't want didn't plan can't afford doesn't love you or go bankrupt or lose a limb or become paralysed or lost at sea or eaten by dogs wolves worms Minotaurs or kidnapped by aliens from outer space or is unpopular at parties has bad breath crotch rot dirty nails smelly feet BO toe jam scaly skin belly-button lint pimples dandruff warts boils nose hair or burps or farts or stutters or sweats is not quick on the up-take or to take advantage is left in the wings in the Lurch at the church falls in love with the wrong person or the right person but the wrong time or the right person at the right time but in the wrong way worried the right person is really not the right person wondering why you want the wrong person knowing they are wrong or someone underage or someone overage or the same sex or an animal rather doing it with zucchini banana cucumber a cored apple eggplant or watermelon missing a car payment a period a joke fear of rats in the Coke bottle poison in the aspirin glass in the sand shit in the Grass strangers in the street on a bus fear of what's under the bed who's in the closet fear of the dark fear of cats spiders snakes bees toads lizards bats purses bridges staircases knives doors foreign films fear of mayonnaise fear of what you did didn't do might've done fear of what you think what you don't think what you think others think what you think others think you think what you think others think about what you think others think you think what you think about thinking about what you think others think about what you think others think about what you think others think about what you think others think you think...

What kinda music you turned on to?
Walls bother me & locks.
Fire & water confuse me I take earth & air for granted
  am distrustful of inanimate objects.
I have an uncanny sense of the graceful line
  so do my best to avoid it. I prefer,
always, the dark horse. Widdershins.
I am too intelligent to be a success or find a steady job.
I cut & paste bits & pieces of what-nots
  to thingamajigs or hammer out doomahickies
    & whatchamacallits for thingamabobs
      (large & small)
    plus an occasional

  whatsahoozie.

There are worse ways to spend one's time.
My family is well.
I love a woman who loves me in return.
& thanks to Herr Freud I can still claim
  dissatisfaction with a clear conscience.
Things are actually quite pleasant.
When I ask whether I am awake or mirrorly dream
  that I am awake, I am answered:
    'Mu'.
Which makes about as much sense as.
Anything.

SCORING

Whatever else a poem
Is always about writing
A poem. Like baseball is about baseball
& hockey, hockey.
The players lining up & the forward
        knowing to drop the puck back
                or shoot for the goal.
Just as the poet lines up words
Choosing one image over another.
Just as freedom is contained
        by rules of play
                & sheet size
Form & style meaning as much to a player as
Content-
Ment
To a group of fans who barely scratch
The icy surface.
Where a blue line only
Always signals
SHOOT!

                [Scores my first hockey poem]

SUNKEN TREASURES

Retired to a secure shore.
No ship coming in to rescue eyes
      hardened by the glare of a thousand coiled suns.
Cracked in the face of it.
Diamond brains squeezed to coal between the hot hands
      of the skull. A surface
where words are required to render the rough beast.
Concrete.
Somehow arriving at the green nocean of a treasured burying.
Matter-of-fact fossilizing further & further
                                          down
                                    Gorgonian
                              stairs
secreting precious coral & no cause to interfere.
Nothing so natural in our nature.
Believing one aquarium safely replicates another.
That goldfish are merely food for pirhana
      that never challenge a pen of liquid glass.
That every oyster contains a pearl.
That all things rise to them that wait.
Bemused by thoughts of a simple gathering along a moonlit beach
Without the weight to imprint sand. Without
the guts to shake a trilobite from its chiselled place.
Flotsam & jetsam cast from wrecks sunk beyond alchemy.
Afraid, even, to rub a lesson from the cold shoulders
      of glacial fish
            that refuse to recognize the impossibility
of their own deep reflections.

It is death, this sea, that offers no translation
      for landlubbers lacking the art of reaching bottom.
Only dissolution & rust beneath the chuck. & above,

a mirror
    bordered by snakes
maintains its

    stony
    design

PS:

'When I retire,' said the lawyer,
'I'm going to write poetry.'
'Isn't that funny,' said the poet.
'When I retire, I'm going to practice law.'

BUZZ BUZZ

No desire beneath these immemorial elms
Outside the insistent buzz of bee-ing.
Nothing too abstract. Real bees in a real
        unfucking tree.
O, (upon this faint reflection)
Kneel. Or not.
Incest breeding a hairy contempt
        for bowlegged boys.
Those further fathers of the man.
Grown blue with ice that never melts.
Footprints appear before the first steps are taken.
Journeying
3
Sheets to the wind
The long day swallows into night.
Buzzes.

IMPROVISATION ON A LINE BY FOUCAULT

What use is a past beyond all use?
Whether Moodie, Orpheus or God.
'The mere possibility of a false bottom opens,
    for those who listen, a space of infinite uncertainty.'
Moebius riding bareback in a 3-ring palindrome
    ensures an eternal strange loop
        meeting itself coming & going
Even as the number 3 rattles water from its horsey wings
    & riddles children's tales with mystery.
Orpheus (I always forget)
Sunk
Without the grace of an egg
Off the shores of Newfoundland.
Poisoning the waters with secrets for years to come.
Broke into pieces no God could re-
Member.
Unlike Moodie who lit way past the Irish, the cholera
& the sea. Had to be unearthed with no trace
    of titanic scratched into her frozen belly.
Spooking woods that wailed
    with the dismembered voice of fire
        & faces that grew out of the tangled foliage.
Giving herself the willies knowing
    a sacrificed dog tossed into a glacial crevasse
        had little effect on ice with a mind to move.
Met head-on suffering a split any
Lyre
Wood
Entrance.

DEATH BY WATER

Death by water impacts the brain with dull ice.
So slow moving, they said,
    it would take a million years.
Just the same, swallowed by a hole
    this natural number subtracted
        instantly
            into the sum of two cubes.
Froze.
To the outline of the skin.
Where a tangled mix of juiceless roots
    sought some hoary fracture in which to operate.
The man with the funnel on his head.
The woman clutching the holy book.
The leech with the drill set to bore & drain
the devilled chunk.
The sculptor armed to chip & chop whatever pieces
failed to fit.
Arguing the pros & cons:

    If one stick of TNT is good
    10 sticks are ten times better &
    100 sticks are ten times better again …

Their shadows dancing across the block.
Sorely amazed as the block
    & the block within the block
        dissolves into a single cloudy puddle
barely big enuf to fill a jar & label:

PETER/1729

Religiously storing it in the cellar
    on a shelf
        somewhere between
            the canned salmon &
pickled pig's feet.

PHANTOM LIMB

for my father

When unreason swells with blood.
Chop off its feet.
Or a life outside the actual is levelled at the knees.
Who refused to turn 40 gracefully
    staggered so far from the knives
        they brought him down reeling
            on the back stroke.
Carries his legs in a suitcase.
Surely this is the symbol of a man.
Tucked away in hospital corners visited by shadows.
Smoking silently.
Waiting.
Inhaling one can almost make out a face.
Or the bare particle flickering in & out of ashes
    like a phantom limb still feels
a pain below the ankle, moaning:

There's an old man in the toilet who can't wash
himself can't sit himself on the crapper can't
wipe his own fartin' arse.

A life squared-off with dragons
    can imagine nothing
Less
Real.

BOARDWALK

These are the lovers.
Threading their way between lake & city.
Alone. Coupled. In groups.
Heat has brought them here.
Along with dogs & children. Cigarettes
& ice cream. They carry themselves in shapes.
Oddly. & these shapes carry shapes
as a single hat transfers from one head to another
in passing. Like bits of conversation we pick up:
    'I just told him, look, HAHAAAA, YOU GOTTA BE KIDDING!
    more money than brains, so I JIMMY! JAMES RUSSELL
    LEWIS WHAT DID I TELL YOU? The way it goes HAHAAAA
    I know it don't look like rain But I heard FUCK 'EM IF THEY
    CAN'T TAKE A JOKE they should trade the guy HAHAAAA.'
French, Italian, German, Spanish, Hungarian, Swahili.
The boardwalk renders all language transparent
& day gives way to night without thot or insistence
comfortable in the Zen-like knowledge that
blackness is the form of forms.
Here objects call attention to themselves.
Not for their 'SIGNIFICANCE', but,
for their significance.
Where the single hair on the mummy of an Egyptian princess
has uncanny evocative power every tree & rock, smell & sound,
move & gesture re-asserts its unique identity.
Performing in concert creates a sum greater than its parts.
A finite number of boards produces a strip of limitless
geography. For us. The lovers.
Facing out across the lake to no horizon, no end.
Only the warm caress of stars to enter into.

THE MOTH POEM

for Lorine Niedecker

A bit of life in the country wot?
How's your oil heater now?
Why shd it refuse to work?
Eating.
An egg.
Froze.
In the fridge.
Anyway.
Smacking the ketchup bottle's.
Bottom.
To release the cap.
& pour.
Over the.
Baked.
Beans.
Some highway, eh?
With stop signs erected at no intersection.
Better luck rubbing with the hard edge of a coin.
Animals emerge from such dense foliage.
A fish becomes a lizard becomes a crow.
In the rear view mirror
    what I thot to be the blown remnant of a tire
        suddenly took flight.
But no. That was another thing entirely.
& nowhere spelt backwards is a novel some
    butler
        pressed between the petals of a rose.
That thing that burns & doesn't outside a bush
from the pages of a dusty book.
Drives insects.
Wild.
Much like music from a comb & tissue.
Distance hesitates at the edge.

A mosquito self-combusts.
Water has bones in this place. Swimming
among fish too long neighbours with the dead.
White beach.
Dear diary.

Woke to six inches of quiet snow. The windows mantled in ice. Listened to a concert on the radio. Saxophone playing a whole solo on 'A-train' composed of tiny quotes from other tunes. Framing a message thru the static. The batteries dying. Died. There was no wood. No water in the pail. No moon in the water. We burned the books & watched the beans bubble on the stove. Snow climbed the sides of the cabin. The wind shivered thru cracks. The fire sucked oxygen & sent its heat gurgling up the pipe. We huddled. Didn't speak. Felt our bodies devilled by the flames. Then came the visions: Sh! Tom sees moths.

MAPPING

I am a coast person
whose only interest in the sea is definition.
Ragged at the edges of this flat form.
Blue & pink penetrate
to breed a colony of cattle stuck knee-deep in the mud.
It appears natural. This process.
What is brutely labelled destiny or weather.
& nothing remains aside from bodies
bloated stubborn with death
& nowhere to dig a hole or mark a grave
as survivors battle each other
with hooves & teeth
for a patch of dry land.

The Chilcotin & Thompson feed the mighty Fraser flushing an estimated 2.2 billion tons of silt annually through the country from as far away as any mountains we might conceive: Coast, Purcell, Selkirk, Monashee, Cariboo & Rockies choking the Strait of Georgia with thousands of soon-to-disappear alluvial islands.

Impossible to keep an updated map
or prevent the liquid shift of landscape.
When one place sinks easily into another.
Name it.
In bold, black letters.
That city dangling at the mouth of that river.

SIGNALS

A thing moves or doesn't.
Is or isn't.
Nothing fuzzy in these branches
    with one foot in & one foot out.
This is irregardless.
Like some gasoline trucks used to read:

    INFLAMMABLE

Could not prevent all hell breaking loose
    converging with a second vehicle in the centre
        of an intersection at 90 miles per hour, whether
Red, Yellow or Green.
Def'n having more to do with
    how a thing behaves in a given flaming instant

Than what we name it.
Burns.

SELF-PORTRAIT

The painting arose partly out of my reading the work of Roy Campbell … introduction to his work by T.S. Eliot …

– Alex Colville

In this painting the horse is given preference.
Which is the way with tragic figures.
Destined to gallop headlong across the ties
        unsoftly into that harsh light
                toward closed
        parallel
Death.
Framed by twin rails so steeped in tradition
        there is no thought that favours perspective.
Still. At this juncture
        (where steam freezes
                & hooves never touch the ground)
One stares amazed & believes
/almost/
The guts of this crazy.
Fucker.
That obscures the real.
Cold villain.
Identifying nowhere.
All
Loco
Motive
Force
Vanishes

CITY OF ANGELS

Illusions linger.
Like, the hot air warps light
    as rain or a phantom sea rising above the sand.
Where the low-throated boom of shifting dunes
    or the red sudden brilliance
        of a vermilion flycatcher put to flight
Seems oddly natural.
Boundaries disappear & the tracks of a caribou
    could as easily be the tracks of a lion or a dinosaur.
Except there are no caribou.
One day near Mount Assiniboine I went across the desert
    just to stare into the Great Slave Aqueduct & recount
        a litany of names connected by sweat & steel:

The Slave River flowing into the Peace, the Peace joining the Little Smoky, then the Berland, the Athabasca, the McLeod, the Pembina, the North Saskatchewan, the Red Deer, the Bow, the Oldman & finally the Flathead, losing the train rushing further south into Idaho.

Contrast the snaking pit of cool, dark water with
    the sere desert plain all around, nearly white with
        the savage sun of an August afternoon.
Hear. The captivating sounds of rushing water
    headed for LA.
The City of Angels.
Seeming utterly
Magical.

THE GORGON

The prime value of historical knowledge is that it is so wonderfully efficacious for disengaging the individual from his own culture & its values.

– Morse Peckham

Impossible to divide a thing by halves & halves
Arriving at an end
Alexander with one sharp blow
Transfigured the mystery
Did not solve it.
Faced with a nest of snakes
Prophetic as Medusa
He gorged on foreign soil
Until he himself was rock.
No end to this thread
That refuses to crystallize
But re-shapes its telling
Knot
By tangled
Knot

Typeset in Myriad and printed at
the Coach House on bpNichol Lane, 1999.

The paper is Zephyr Antique Laid.

Editor for the Press: Victor Coleman.

To read the online version of this text and other titles from Coach House Books, or to order any of our titles, visit our website:

www.chbooks.com

To add your name to our e-mailing list, write:
mail@chbooks.com

Toll-free:
1 800 367 6360

Coach House Books
401 Huron Street (rear) on bpNichol Lane
Toronto, Ontario M5S 2G5